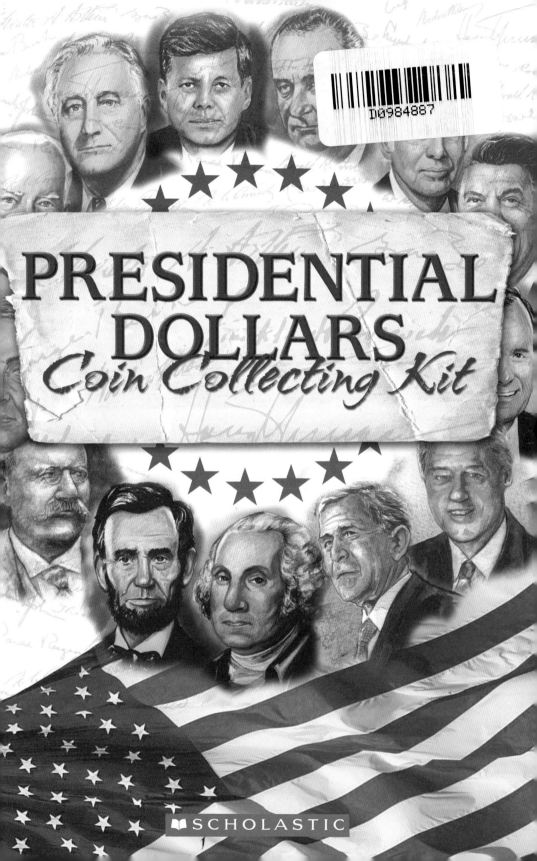

PRESIDENTIAL DOLLARS
Coin Collecting Kit

SCHOLASTIC

Written by Tammi Salzano
Illustrated by Daniel Jankowski
Designed by Deena Fleming

Copyright © 2007 Scholastic Inc.

an imprint of
■SCHOLASTIC
www.scholastic.com

Scholastic and Tangerine Press and associated logos are
trademarks of Scholastic Inc.

Published by Tangerine Press, an imprint of
Scholastic Inc., 557 Broadway; New York, NY 10012

10 9 8 7 6 5 4 3

ISBN-10: 0-545-03814-6
ISBN-13: 978-0-545-03814-0

Printed and bound in China

PRESIDENTIAL DOLLARS
Coin Collecting Kit

Contents

"Ladies and Gentlemen, the President of the United States."

The office of the president of the United States is one of the most recognizable, powerful jobs in the world. The president is responsible for making important decisions that affect not only the United States, but other countries as well. The Presidential $1 Coin Act of 2005 was passed to honor the presidents, now deceased, who have served our great nation as leader. Each president was eligible to appear on a dollar coin two years after his death. You can begin your coin collection by keeping the presidential coins in the folder that came in your kit. Four coins are issued each year beginning in 2007, so be on the lookout to add to your collection.

Inside this book, you'll find historical information about all of the presidents, as well as interesting facts that you won't find in any textbook. Read on to find out which president was an excellent marbles player, which one had a pet raccoon, who liked to paint by numbers, and much more!

George Washington

1st

"I hope I shall possess firmness and virtue enough to maintain what I consider the most enviable of all titles, the character of an honest man."

A Life in Brief

George Washington became a land surveyor at age 15, and at 21, the United States' first president was a military spy for the British army! He became the commander in chief of the Continental Army during the American Revolution and president of the Constitutional Convention. He was elected unanimously to the office of the president, the only president to claim that honor. Known for his honesty and fairness, Washington established important precedents during his presidency. One was for the United States to remain neutral in foreign conflicts, and another was to limit the president's time in office to two terms. (An exception was Franklin D. Roosevelt, the 32nd president, who was elected to four terms.) Slavery was commonplace during Washington's presidency, and even though he was a plantation owner, he eventually freed all his slaves, becoming the only Founding Father to do so.

Did You Know?

* Washington was the first president to appear on a postage stamp.

* He carried a portable sundial.

* The population of the United States was close to four million when Washington was elected. Today, there are nearly 300 million people in the country.

* His likeness appears on the $1 bill.

* Many people think that Washington had wooden false teeth, but that's untrue. He did, however, have a set of false teeth made from iron, one made from ivory, and a set made from extracted human teeth!

* He loved ice cream so much that he installed two ice-cream freezers at his home, Mount Vernon.

* He loved to go fox hunting.

* Washington had six white horses, and he ordered their teeth brushed every morning.

* After Washington died, his wife, Martha, burned all of his letters to preserve her husband's privacy.

* Washington had to borrow money to attend his own inauguration.

* He used to crack nuts with his teeth, which is why he needed so many sets of false ones. By the time he was elected president, he had only one natural tooth left in his mouth. His inaugural speech was a brief 90 seconds because his dentures didn't fit him very well, and it was difficult for him to speak.

Born:
February 22, 1732
Birthplace:
Westmoreland County, Virginia
Political Party:
Federalist
Term of Office:
April 30, 1789–
March 3, 1797
Vice President:
John Adams
First Lady:
Martha Dandridge Custis Washington, his wife
Nickname:
Father of Our Country
Died:
December 14, 1799

Washington taking command of the American army under the old elm at Cambridge, July 3, 1775

Washington's room, Washington's headquarters at Ford Mansion, Morristown, N.J.

"I Cannot Tell a Lie"

George Washington is known for a famous story in which his father asked him if he chopped down a cherry tree in the yard. Washington supposedly responded that yes, he did chop it down with his hatchet. There's no historical evidence to support that the story is true, and many historians believe that it was created to show Washington's honesty.

John Adams

A Life in Brief

John Adams was a teacher, lawyer, and surveyor. He successfully defended the British soldiers who were accused of murder during the trial of the Boston Massacre in 1770. Early in his presidency, Adams urged the country to separate from Great Britain, which had control at that time. He is credited with creating the Department of the Navy and organizing the Marine Corps. Adams was one of the signers of the Declaration of Independence in 1776, which freed the original 13 colonies from the rule of Great Britain.

John Adams

"Liberty cannot be preserved without a general knowledge among the people."

2nd

Born:
October 20, 1735

Birthplace:
Braintree (now Quincy), Massachusetts

Political Party:
Federalist

Term of Office:
March 4, 1797–
March 3, 1801

Vice President:
Thomas Jefferson

First Lady:
Abigail Smith Adams, his wife

Nickname:
Father of the American Navy

Died:
July 4, 1826

Did You Know?

★ Adams was the first president to live in the White House (then called the Executive Mansion).

★ During his presidency, the capital of the country was moved to Washington, D.C.

★ Adams and his wife, Abigail, used the East Room of the White House as a place for hanging laundry to dry.

★ He hated to study Latin and asked his father for another work assignment. His father assigned him to digging a ditch in a meadow. After two days of digging, Adams happily went back to studying Latin.

★ Adams once stole a sliver of wood from a chair at William Shakespeare's birthplace as a souvenir.

★ He attempted unsuccessfully to lobby the Senate of the first Congress to make the presidency a royal, inherited position.

★ Intent on leaving his mark on the next administration, Adams spent the final hours of his presidency appointing officials in what became known as the Midnight Appointments.

Thomas Jefferson

Thomas Jefferson wrote the first draft of the Declaration of Independence. Though a lawyer by profession, over the course of his lifetime he was governor of Virginia, minister to France, secretary of state, vice president, and president. As president, Jefferson authorized the purchase of the Louisiana territory from France for $.04 an acre, doubling the size of the country. He then sent Lewis and Clark on their famous expedition to explore the land.

Th Jefferson

3rd

"We hold these truths to be self-evident: that all men are created equal; that they are endowed by their Creator with certain unalienable rights; that among these are life, liberty, and the pursuit of happiness."

Did You Know?

★ Jefferson was the first president to shake hands with people instead of bowing to them.

★ His likeness appears on the nickel coin.

★ He had a pet mockingbird named Dick who liked to ride on his shoulder.

★ Jefferson played the violin.

★ He took a cold footbath every morning for 60 years.

★ Jefferson invented many devices that are still in use today, such as the swivel chair. He believed that everyone should benefit from inventions, so he never patented any of them.

★ He often entertained dinner guests in old homespun clothes and bedroom slippers.

★ He was a paleontologist (someone who studies fossils). One species of extinct giant sloth, the *Megalonyx jeffersonii*, is named in honor of him.

Born:
April 13, 1743
Birthplace:
Shadwell, Virginia
Political Party:
Democratic-Republican
Term of Office:
March 4, 1801–
March 3, 1809
Vice Presidents:
Aaron Burr (1801–05),
George Clinton
(1805–09)
First Lady:
Martha "Patsy"
Randolph, his daughter
Nickname:
Father of the
Declaration of
Independence
Died:
July 4, 1826

James Madison

A Life in Brief

James Madison is perhaps most well known for drafting the Bill of Rights, which are the first ten Amendments to the Constitution and which spell out the rights of the individual citizen. He served as secretary of state under Thomas Jefferson and was a member of the Continental Congress. Madison joined Alexander Hamilton and John Jay in writing The Federalist Papers, which were created to help gain popular support for the states' ratification of the Constitution.

4th

James Madison

"A pure democracy is a society consisting of a small number of citizens, who assemble and administer the government in person."

Born:
March 16, 1751
Birthplace:
Port Conway, Virginia
Political Party:
Democratic-Republican
Term of Office:
March 4, 1809–
March 3, 1817
Vice Presidents:
George Clinton
(1809–13), Elbridge
Gerry (1813–17)
First Lady:
Dolley Payne Todd
Madison, his wife
Nickname:
Father of the
Constitution
Died:
June 28, 1836

Did You Know?

★ Madison graduated from Princeton University in only two years.

★ He was the shortest president at five feet, four inches tall.

★ He was the first president to wear long trousers.

★ The capital of Wisconsin is named for Madison.

★ At age 29, Madison was the youngest member of the Continental Congress.

★ It was during Madison's presidency that the Executive Mansion was first called the White House.

★ He supported the gradual abolition of slavery.

★ During the War of 1812, the British entered Washington, D.C., and set the White House on fire.

★ Madison's wife, Dolley, organized the first annual Easter Egg Roll on the Capitol grounds.

James Monroe

James Monroe (signature)

James Monroe became a lieutenant colonel in the Continental army at age 20. He studied law and was a member of the Continental Congress and the U.S. Senate. He served as minister to France and Great Britain and negotiated the Louisiana Purchase before buying Florida from Spain, further expanding America's territory. He created the Monroe Doctrine, warning Europe to leave the Western Hemisphere alone. Despite a serious economic recession from 1819 to 1821, Monroe's presidency was described as "The Era of Good Feelings" because of the nation's growth and optimism.

"If we look to the history of other nations, ancient or modern, we find no example of a growth so rapid, so gigantic, of a people so prosperous and happy."

5th

Did You Know?

⭐ Monroe spoke fluent French and preferred it to English.

⭐ He was the only president wounded in the Revolutionary War.

⭐ He was so popular that no one ran against him for reelection.

⭐ The first wedding performed in the White House was the marriage of Monroe's daughter Marie Hester.

⭐ During his presidency, nine stars were added to the United States flag.

⭐ Monroe was the first president to ride a steamboat.

⭐ He was stripped of his duties as minister to France when he failed to obey George Washington's orders.

⭐ Monroe left office in debt and resorted to living with his daughter in New York City.

Born:
April 28, 1758
Birthplace:
Westmoreland County, Virginia
Political Party:
Democratic-Republican
Term of Office:
March 4, 1817–
March 3, 1825
Vice President:
Daniel D. Tompkins
First Lady:
Elizabeth Kortright Monroe, his wife
Nickname:
The Last Cocked Hat
Died:
July 4, 1831

John Quincy Adams

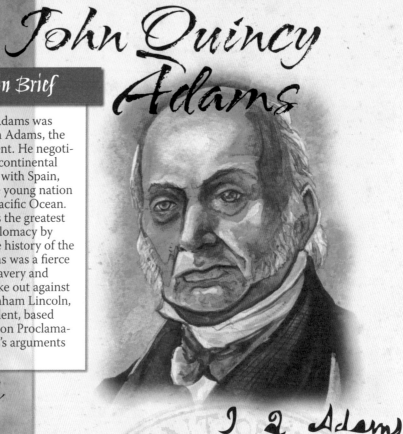

A Life in Brief

John Quincy Adams was the son of John Adams, the second president. He negotiated the Transcontinental Treaty of 1819 with Spain, which gave the young nation access to the Pacific Ocean. This treaty was the greatest triumph in diplomacy by one man in the history of the country! Adams was a fierce opponent of slavery and frequently spoke out against it. In fact, Abraham Lincoln, the 16th president, based his Emancipation Proclamation on Adams's arguments against slavery.

6th

J. Q. Adams

"America, with the same voice which spoke herself into existence as a nation, proclaimed to mankind the inextinguishable rights of human nature, and the only lawful foundations of government."

Born:
July 11, 1767

Birthplace:
Braintree (now Quincy), Massachusetts

Political Party:
Democratic-Republican

Term of Office:
March 4, 1825–
March 3, 1829

Vice President:
John C. Calhoun

First Lady:
Louisa Catherine Johnson, his wife

Nickname:
Old Man Eloquent

Died:
February 23, 1848

Did You Know?

★ Adams was the first president whose father had been president.

★ He was the first president to marry a foreign-born woman. His wife, Louisa, was born in England.

★ He kept a diary for more than 60 years.

★ Adams had the first billiards table installed in the White House.

★ He named one of his sons George Washington.

★ He put little effort into his appearance and reportedly wore the same hat for 10 years.

★ He liked to swim nude in the Potomac River and once had to ask a stranger to bring him clothes from the White House when boys stole the ones that he'd removed.

Andrew Jackson

A Life in Brief

Andrew Jackson, a lawyer and military man by profession, served in both the Revolutionary War and the War of 1812. He won crucial victories as a major general in the latter and was propelled into politics. He was the first governor of the Florida Territory and served in the U.S. Senate. Jackson is also credited with founding the Democratic Party, one of the country's major political organizations.

7th

Andrew Jackson

"One man with courage makes a majority."

Did You Know?

⭐ At age nine, Jackson learned public speaking skills and read newspapers to people who couldn't read.

⭐ He was the first president to ride a railroad train.

⭐ He was the first president to be nominated by a political party, which established the precedent in place today.

⭐ His likeness appears on the $20 bill.

⭐ Jackson is the only president to pay off the national debt.

⭐ During his first inaugural celebration, supporters stormed the White House, tracking in mud, damaging furniture, and starting fights.

⭐ Jackson once threw a party in the White House and served a 1,400-pound wheel of cheese.

⭐ He lived with a bullet lodged within two inches of his heart, the result of a duel.

⭐ At Jackson's funeral, his pet parrot had to be taken out of the room because it was swearing.

Born:
March 15, 1767
Birthplace:
Waxhaw area, on North Carolina–South Carolina border
Political Party:
Democratic
Term of Office:
March 4, 1829–
March 3, 1837
Vice Presidents:
John C. Calhoun (1829–32), Martin Van Buren (1833–37)
First Lady:
Emily Donelson, niece of his wife, Rachel
Nickname:
Old Hickory
Died:
June 8, 1845

13

Martin Van Buren

A Life in Brief

Martin Van Buren became a lawyer by the age of 20. He began his political career as a minor county official, but he quickly earned the public's respect as a capable politician. Before assuming the presidency, Van Buren served as a member of the U.S. Senate and governor of New York. He was also vice president and secretary of state under Andrew Jackson. It was his promise to carry on Jackson's policies at the end of Jackson's term that won him the presidential election of 1836.

8th

"There is a power in public opinion in this country—and I thank God for it: for it is the most honest and best of all powers—which will not tolerate an incompetent or unworthy man to hold in his weak or wicked hands the lives and fortunes of his fellow-citizens."

Born:
December 5, 1782
Birthplace:
Kinderhook, New York
Political Party:
Democratic
Term of Office:
March 4, 1837–
March 3, 1841
Vice President:
Richard M. Johnson
First Lady:
Angelica Singleton
Van Buren, his
daughter-in-law
Nickname:
Little Magician
Died:
July 24, 1862

Did You Know?

★ Van Buren was the first president born in the new United States.

★ He opposed making Texas a state.

★ Van Buren raised four sons on his own after his wife died.

★ He enjoyed an expensive lifestyle. When an economic crisis known as the Panic of 1837 hit, he continued in his lavish ways and was viewed by many as a rich man who didn't care about the country's poor.

★ He ordered that 20,000 Cherokee Indians move from the eastern states to Oklahoma in what became known as the Trail of Tears. More than 5,000 people died on the journey.

William Henry Harrison

William Henry Harrison was born into a rich, political family. He served as territorial governor of present-day Indiana and Illinois, a position he held for 12 years. Harrison was a military man, earning the reputation among white settlers as an Indian fighter. As a general, he spearheaded the defeat of Tecumseh and the Shawnees at the Battle of Tippecanoe in the Ohio River Valley in 1811, which made him a national hero. Harrison served as a member of the U.S. Senate prior to being chosen as a presidential candidate by the Whigs, the same name as the British party that was opposed to the monarchy.

"But I contend that the strongest of all governments is that which is most free."

9th

Did You Know?

⭐ Harrison and his wife had 10 children.

⭐ As governor, Harrison was responsible for purchasing over 50 million acres of land for $2,550. The Shawnees felt that they had been duped and retaliated, sparking the Battle of Tippecanoe.

⭐ He was the first president to have a campaign slogan—"Tippecanoe and Tyler, too."

⭐ Anna Symmes Harrison was the first president's wife to have a formal education.

⭐ He was the grandfather of future president Benjamin Harrison.

⭐ He opposed limiting the power that slaveholders had over their slaves and rejected efforts to stop slavery.

⭐ Harrison gave a record two-hour inaugural speech in the rain. He developed pneumonia and died after serving only 32 days, becoming the first president to die in office.

Born:
February 9, 1773
Birthplace:
Charles City County, Virginia
Political Party:
Whig
Term of Office:
March 4, 1841 –
April 4, 1841
Vice President:
John Tyler
First Lady:
Jane Irwin Harrison, his daughter-in-law
Nickname:
Old Tippecanoe
Died:
April 4, 1841

John Tyler

John Tyler was governor of Virginia and served in the U.S. House of Representatives and the U.S. Senate. He became the first vice president to achieve the presidency because of the death of the elected president. During his term, Texas was annexed as both a slave and free state. In 1844, Tyler signed a treaty with China that opened up trade with the United States.

10th

John Tyler

"So far as it depends on the course of this government, our relations of good will and friendship will be sedulously cultivated with all nations."

Born:
March 29, 1790

Birthplace:
Charles City County, Virginia

Political Party:
Democratic

Term of Office:
April 6, 1841–
March 3, 1845

Vice President:
None

First Ladies:
Priscilla Cooper Tyler, his daughter-in-law;
Julia Gardiner Tyler, his second wife

Nickname:
Accidental President

Died:
January 18, 1862

Did You Know?

⭐ Tyler was the first president to be widowed and remarried while in office.

⭐ He had the most children of any president (15).

⭐ Tyler fathered his last child at the age of 70.

⭐ He was threatened with impeachment by both the Whigs and the Democratic Party.

⭐ Tyler's wife, Julia, started the tradition of playing "Hail to the Chief" when the president entered the room.

⭐ He vetoed a bill to reestablish the Bank of the United States. His entire cabinet, except for one man, resigned. The Whigs demanded his resignation and expelled him from the party.

⭐ Tyler was known as a political outlaw and was the first president to have a veto overridden by Congress.

⭐ He gave up his U.S. citizenship when he was elected to the Confederate House of Representatives in 1861.

James K. Polk

A Life in Brief

James Knox Polk was Speaker of the U.S. House of Representatives. He learned much about politics from his good friend Andrew Jackson. Polk acquired California, New Mexico, and Texas with victory in the Mexican War in 1848. He also claimed Nevada, Wyoming, Utah, and Arizona, the biggest addition of land since the Louisiana Purchase.

James K. Polk

11th

"Peace, plenty, and contentment reign throughout our borders, and our beloved country presents a sublime moral spectacle to the world."

Did You Know?

★ Polk was the first "dark horse" political party candidate, which means that he was an unexpected nominee.

★ He was the first president who did not seek reelection.

★ He was president when the California Gold Rush began in 1849.

★ At age 14, had abdominal surgery without anesthesia.

★ Polk liked to wear his hair long.

★ He and his wife, Sarah, did not have any children.

★ His wife did not allow dancing in the White House.

★ As president, Polk failed to do anything about social problems of the time, such as slavery, immigrants living in poverty, and children working in factories.

★ Polk's wife replaced all of the servants in the White House with slaves and housed them in cramped sleeping quarters in the basement.

Born:
November 2, 1795
Birthplace:
Mecklenburg County, North Carolina
Political Party:
Democratic
Term of Office:
March 4, 1845–
March 3, 1849
Vice President:
George M. Dallas
First Lady:
Sarah Childress Polk, his wife
Nickname:
Young Hickory
Died:
June 15, 1849

17

Zachary Taylor

A Life in Brief

Zachary Taylor was a soldier for 40 years. One of his greatest achievements prior to becoming president was his victory over General Santa Anna in the Mexican War in 1845. Severely outnumbered 20,000 to 6,000, Taylor's army defeated the Mexican force, and Taylor became a national hero.

12th

Zachary Taylor

> "My life has been devoted to arms, yet I look upon war at all times and under any circumstances as a national calamity to be avoided if compatible with National Honor."

Did You Know?

Born:
November 24, 1784
Birthplace:
near Barboursville, Virginia
Political Party:
Whig
Term of Office:
March 4, 1849–
July 9, 1850
Vice President:
Millard Fillmore
First Lady:
Betty Taylor Bliss, his daughter
Nickname:
Old Rough and Ready
Died:
July 9, 1850

★ During his career as a military commander, Taylor never lost a battle.

★ He was so short that he had to be boosted into his saddle.

★ He was the first president who had not previously served as an elected official in any public office.

★ Taylor had an unusual style of dress and frequently mixed military and civilian clothes.

★ His oldest daughter married Jefferson Davis, who went on to become president of the Confederacy.

★ His only son served as a general in the Confederate army.

★ Taylor never voted or belonged to a political party until he ran for president when he was 62 years old.

★ He had a horse named Old Whitey, who was part of his funeral procession.

★ Taylor's wife vowed not to go into society if her husband returned home safely from the Mexican War. When he did, she kept her promise. His daughter assumed the role of First Lady.

Millard Fillmore

Millard Fillmore was a member of the U.S. House of Representatives and served as both a congressman and the comptroller of the state of New York. As president, he authorized Matthew Perry's trip to Japan, which helped open up trade with that country. He signed the Compromise of 1850, which kept the country from civil war for 10 years. The Compromise admitted California to the union as a free state but also enacted the Fugitive Slave Act, which denied suspected fugitives (escaped slaves) the right to a trial.

"God knows that I detest slavery, but it is an existing evil, for which we are not responsible, and we must endure it, till we can get rid of it without destroying the last hope of free government in the world."

13th

Did You Know?

★ Fillmore was born into extreme poverty. In order to help support his family, he was apprenticed by his father to a clothmaker, where he was forced to work 15 hours a day. He finally borrowed enough money to pay his obligation to the clothmaker and walked 100 miles to return home to his family.

★ He taught himself to read.

★ He was 18 years old when he started school. He eventually married his teacher, Abigail Powers.

★ There were 30 states in the United States at the time of Fillmore's presidency.

★ He installed the first bathtub that had running water in the White House.

★ Fillmore brought the first cast-iron stove to the White House, which replaced the fireplace.

★ As First Lady, Abigail Fillmore established the White House library.

★ Fillmore ran unsuccessfully for president in 1856 as a candidate on the Know-Nothing ticket, a party formed to oppose immigration.

Born:
January 7, 1800
Birthplace:
Summerhill, New York
Political Party:
Whig
Term of Office:
July 10, 1850–
March 3, 1853
Vice President:
None
First Lady:
Abigail Fillmore,
his wife
Nickname:
The Compromise
President
Died:
March 8, 1874

Franklin Pierce

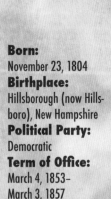

A Life in Brief

Franklin Pierce served as a general during the Mexican War, but his troops had little respect for his military skills. As president, Pierce was responsible for the Gadsden Purchase, which gave the United States the land that's now southern Arizona and southern New Mexico—more than 45,500 square miles of land.

14th

"I believe that involuntary servitude [slavery], as it exists in different States of this Confederacy, is recognized by the Constitution."

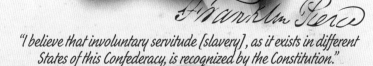

Did You Know?

Born:
November 23, 1804
Birthplace:
Hillsborough (now Hillsboro), New Hampshire
Political Party:
Democratic
Term of Office:
March 4, 1853–
March 3, 1857
Vice President:
William R. D. King
First Lady:
Jane Appleton Pierce, his wife
Nickname:
Fainting Frank
Died:
October 8, 1869

⭐ Pierce was the first president to display a Christmas tree in the White House.

⭐ Each of Pierce's three children died before reaching adolescence.

⭐ His classmates included writers Nathaniel Hawthorne and Henry Wadsworth Longfellow.

⭐ He was the first president to recite his inaugural address from memory.

⭐ Pierce did not campaign to be president. He was nominated by his friends in the Democratic Party and never even gave one campaign speech.

⭐ As an inexperienced general in the Mexican War, Pierce fell from a horse and his leg was crushed. He fainted as a result of the accident and acquired the unfortunate nickname "Fainting Frank."

⭐ Feelings in Congress were so intense during his term that fistfights often broke out on the meeting floor.

⭐ Pierce signed the Kansas–Nebraska Act of 1854, which gave settlers the right to decide whether or not to permit slavery. Kansas became known as "Bloody Kansas" because of the intense fighting that occurred over the slavery issue.

James Buchanan

James Buchanan was a member of the U.S. House of Representatives and the U.S. Senate. He also served as minister to Russia under President Jackson, secretary of state under President Polk, and minister to England under President Pierce. The nation was severely divided over the issue of slavery when Buchanan took office; the northern states wanted to eliminate slavery, while the southern states supported it. Hopes were high that Buchanan could bring the country back together. Instead, the Union broke apart, and at the end of his term, the country faced the threat of civil war.

James Buchanan

"My dear sir, if you are as happy on entering the White House as I on leaving, you are a very happy man indeed." (to Abraham Lincoln)

15th

Did You Know?

- Buchanan was the first president born in Pennsylvania.

- He was engaged to a wealthy woman, but her family opposed the marriage. She died suddenly, and he was not allowed to attend the funeral. He vowed never to marry and was the only president to have never married.

- The king of Siam offered to send Buchanan several pairs of elephants. Abraham Lincoln, the 16th president, politely declined the offer.

- During Buchanan's time in office, he received from Queen Victoria the first telegraph message sent across the Atlantic Ocean.

- Buchanan ran for the presidency four times before finally winning.

- Buchanan did not stop South Carolina, Mississippi, Florida, Alabama, Georgia, and Texas from forming the Confederate States of America.

Born:
April 23, 1791
Birthplace:
Cove Gap (near Mercersburg), Pennsylvania
Political Party:
Democratic
Term of Office:
March 4, 1857–
March 3, 1861
Vice President:
John C. Breckinridge
First Lady:
Harriet Lane, his niece
Nickname:
Old Buck
Died:
June 1, 1868

Abraham Lincoln

16th

Abraham Lincoln

"Four score and seven years ago our fathers brought forth, upon this continent, a new nation, conceived in Liberty, and dedicated to the proposition that all men are created equal."
(Introduction to the Gettysburg Address)

A Life in Brief

Abraham Lincoln is regarded by many historians as the nation's greatest president. He saw the country through the Civil War, all the while promising to reunite the states after the North's victory over the South. He was an outspoken opponent of slavery, and halfway through the war, he issued the Emancipation Proclamation, which freed three million slaves. This single act changed the war from a battle to preserve the union to a battle for freedom. Victory by Union forces in 1865 established forever the principle that the federal government's authority is stronger than states' rights. Lincoln also gave one of the most famous speeches in American history, the Gettysburg Address, in which he stressed equality and respect for every citizen.

⭐ Lincoln was the first president born outside of the original 13 colonies.

⭐ He had less than one year of formal schooling.

⭐ He grew up extremely poor. He loved books and taught himself law.

⭐ When he was 19 years old, he built a flatboat and brought farm produce down the Mississippi River from Illinois to New Orleans. He then sold the boat for timber and walked home—more than 800 miles!—and gave his earnings to his father.

⭐ Lincoln was the first Republican president.

⭐ He was the tallest president at six feet, four inches tall.

⭐ There are five known manuscript copies of the Gettysburg Address, two of which are housed at the Library of Congress.

⭐ During Lincoln's campaign for president, an 11-year-old girl told Lincoln that he should grow a beard because his face was so thin. She told him that a beard would make him more appealing. He took her advice, and the rest is history.

⭐ Lincoln was the first president to use the draft to supply men for the Army.

⭐ He was a great marbles player and often played for relaxation during the Civil War.

⭐ He was the first president to use "greenbacks," or paper money.

⭐ Lincoln was the first president to implement the income tax.

⭐ Wrestling was one of his favorite sports.

⭐ He appointed Andrew Johnson (the 17th president) the military governor of Tennessee. Shortly thereafter, Johnson convinced Lincoln to exempt Tennessee from the Emancipation Proclamation.

⭐ He asked Robert E. Lee to command the Union army, but Lee chose to serve with the Confederacy instead.

⭐ Lincoln was the first president to be assassinated. He was shot and killed in Ford's Theater in Washington, D.C., by John Wilkes Booth.

President Lincoln and Sojourner Truth at the Executive Mansion, Washington, D.C., Oct. 29, 1864

Born:
February 12, 1809
Birthplace:
Hardin (now Larue) County, Kentucky
Political Party:
Republican
Term of Office:
March 4, 1861 –
April 15, 1865
Vice Presidents:
Hannibal Hamlin (March 4, 1861 –
March 3, 1865),
Andrew Johnson (March 4 –
April 15, 1865)
First Lady:
Mary Todd Lincoln, his wife.
Nicknames:
The Great Emancipator, Honest Abe
Died:
April 15, 1865

Andrew Johnson

Andrew Johnson was a member of both the U.S. House of Representatives and the Senate. Much of his presidency was marked by chaos and inept leadership. He lost support due to his defense of slavery and his verbal attacks on his political opponents. The first president to be impeached, or brought up on charges to face possible removal from office, Johnson was spared by one vote. Congress overrode his veto on bills to protect the rights of all citizens, including blacks born in the United States.

17th

Andrew Johnson

"Honest conviction is my courage; the Constitution is my guide."

Did You Know?

Born:
December 29, 1808
Birthplace:
Raleigh, North Carolina
Political Party:
Democratic
Term of Office:
April 15, 1865–
March 3, 1869
Vice President:
None
First Lady:
Martha Johnson
Patterson, his daughter
Nickname:
None
Died:
July 31, 1875

★ At age 14, Johnson and his older brother, William, were apprenticed to a tailor but ran away after several years.

★ He did not learn the basics of reading or math until he was 17 years old. His future wife taught him.

★ He made some of his own clothes.

★ His wife, Eliza, was ill and unable to serve as First Lady. Johnson's daughter Martha assumed the role.

★ He was the first president to receive a visit by a queen (Queen Emma of the Sandwich Islands, now Hawaii).

★ He pardoned all Southerners who had fought in the Civil War.

★ William Seward, Johnson's secretary of state, negotiated the purchase of Alaska from Russia at $.02 an acre in what was known as "Seaward's Folly."

★ Johnson was buried with his head resting on his copy of the Constitution.

Ulysses S. Grant

Ulysses Simpson Grant was the leader of the Union troops during the Civil War. He was best known for the Union victory at Appomattox Courthouse, where Robert E. Lee and the Confederate forces surrendered, ending the Civil War. But his popularity and military success did not carry over into his presidency. Grant appointed corrupt, incompetent friends to his cabinet and generally failed at economic policy. He was unable to pull the economy out of the chaos it entered when the Civil War ended.

"I have never advocated war except as a means of peace."

18th

Did You Know?

* Grant was the first president born in Ohio.

* His first name given at birth was Hiram.

* His likeness appears on the $50 bill.

* Grant was the first president elected in part by former slaves.

* During his presidency, the first transcontinental railroad was completed.

* The telephone was invented during his second term of office.

* Grant finished writing his memoirs just two days before he died. Mark Twain helped to get the book published.

* He was forced to resign his commission from the army because of excessive drinking.

* He was fined $20 for speeding through Washington, D.C., in his carriage.

* During his term, the 15th Amendment to the Constitution was ratified, which gave men the right to vote.

* Grant smoked 20 cigars a day and died from throat cancer.

* He is buried in New York City.

Born:
April 27, 1822
Birthplace:
Point Pleasant, Ohio
Political Party:
Republican
Term of Office:
March 4, 1869–
March 3, 1877
Vice Presidents:
Schuyler Colfax
(1869–73), Henry
Wilson (1873–75)
First Lady:
Julia Dent Grant, his wife
Nickname:
Hero of Appomattox
Died:
July 23, 1885

Rutherford B. Hayes

A Life in Brief

Rutherford Birchard Hayes is credited with restoring respect and dignity to the White House in the wake of the Lincoln assassination, the impeachment of Andrew Johnson, and Grant's corrupt administration. Among other key policies, he supported civil service reform and put an end to Congress' ability to pass laws without the president's approval.

19th

"He serves his party best who serves the country best."

Born:
October 4, 1822
Birthplace:
Delaware, Ohio
Political Party:
Republican
Term of Office:
March 4, 1877–
March 3, 1881
Vice President:
William A. Wheeler
First Lady:
Lucy Ware Webb Hayes,
his wife
Nickname:
Dark-Horse President
Died:
January 17, 1893

Did You Know?

★ Hayes won the presidential election by only one electoral vote.

★ He was the first president to have a telephone in the White House.

★ His wife, Lucy, was the first to be referred to as the "First Lady" and also to hold a college degree.

★ Hayes was the first president to take a trip to the West Coast of the United States.

★ His wife was nicknamed "Lemonade Lucy" because she refused to serve alcoholic beverages in the White House.

★ He didn't drink or smoke, even though virtually all men during this time did so.

★ A lawyer by profession, he offered free legal assistance and refuge to escaped slaves.

★ After the Civil War, Hayes ordered the remaining peace-keeping troops out of the South. White supremacists gained power in that region, which resulted in the denial of rights of black Americans for nearly a century.

James A. Garfield

James Abram Garfield is considered a "lost President" due to his generally uneventful term in the White House, which ended when he was shot by an assassin's bullet and died only a few months after taking office. He was a great orator, and prior to taking office, he served in the U.S. House of Representatives. During his presidency, the American Red Cross was established.

J A Garfield

20th

"We cannot overestimate the fervent love of liberty, the intelligent courage, and the sum of common sense with which our fathers made the great experiment of self-government."

Did You Know?

★ Garfield was the last president to be born in a log cabin.

★ He was born into poverty and put himself through college by working as a teacher, carpenter, and janitor.

★ He ran away from home at age 16 and took a job on a canal boat. He fell overboard 14 times and eventually returned home due to seasickness.

★ Garfield studied law on his own and became a lawyer at age 30.

★ He was the first left-handed president.

★ He could write in Latin with one hand and Greek with the other.

★ He was the first president to campaign in two languages, English and German.

★ Garfield's wife, Lucretia, caught malaria from the mosquitoes in the swamps behind the White House but recovered completely.

★ Garfield was shot and killed by a man named Charles Julius Guiteau, who had been denied a role in Garfield's administration and who was later determined to be insane.

Born:
November 19, 1831
Birthplace:
Orange Township, Cuyahoga County, Ohio
Political Party:
Republican
Term of Office:
March 4, 1881 –
September 19, 1881
Vice President:
Chester A. Arthur
First Lady:
Lucretia Rudolph Garfield, his wife
Nickname:
Preacher President
Died:
September 19, 1881

Chester A. Arthur

A Life in Brief

Chester Alan Arthur was a teacher and a lawyer early in his career. At the beginning of the Civil War, he served as quartermaster general of the State of New York. He was a reformer, and as president, he changed the civil service program. He signed the Pendleton Act, which required potential federal employees to take competency exams. He is known as the Father of the Steel Navy because he modernized the Navy by building steel ships.

21st

"Men may die, but the fabrics of our free institutions remain unshaken."

Did You Know?

Born:
October 5, 1829
Birthplace:
Fairfield, Vermont
Political Party:
Republican
Term of Office:
September 20, 1881–
March 3, 1885
Vice President:
None
First Lady:
Mary Arthur McElroy, his sister
Nicknames:
The Gentleman Boss, Elegant Arthur
Died:
November 18, 1886

⭐ Arthur lost his job as collector of the Port of New York after evidence of corruption surfaced.

⭐ He was the first president to hire a valet, or personal servant.

⭐ He was one of three presidents who served in 1881.

⭐ Arthur had more than 80 pairs of pants and changed his clothes several times a day.

⭐ He dedicated the Washington Monument on February 21, 1885.

⭐ His wife, Ellen, died before he became president. He had a stained-glass window, dedicated to her, placed in a church near the White House so that he could see it when he looked out his window.

⭐ After he took office, he learned he had a kidney disease but kept it a secret.

⭐ He signed the Chinese Exclusion Act of 1882, which banned Chinese immigration to the United States for 10 years.

Grover Cleveland

Stephen Grover Cleveland was the mayor of Buffalo, New York, and the governor of New York prior to becoming president. He had a reputation of being honest and hardworking, and once in office, he made it his mission to change the policies that were not working. He is regarded by historians as a president who protected the powers of the office, as he did not attempt to use Congress as a way to get his own agendas passed.

"A government for the people must depend for its success on the intelligence, the morality, the justice, and the interest of the people themselves."

22nd 24th

Did You Know?

⭐ Cleveland avoided being drafted into the Union army by paying a substitute soldier $300 to serve for him.

⭐ An avid hunter, Cleveland and some friends were thought to have been lost when they didn't return from a hunting trip for several days.

⭐ Cleveland's wife, Frances, was 27 years younger than he.

⭐ He was the only president to serve two non-consecutive terms.

⭐ He was the only president to be married in the White House.

⭐ His second child, Esther, was the first child born in the White House.

⭐ Cleveland dedicated the Statue of Liberty during his first term.

⭐ He had an operation on his mouth and had to wear an artificial rubber jaw.

⭐ When Cleveland and his wife left the White House after his first term, she told the staff to take care of the furniture because they would return—which they did, in 1893.

Born:
March 18, 1837
Birthplace:
Caldwell,
New Jersey
Political Party:
Democratic
Terms of Office:
March 4, 1885–
March 3, 1889;
March 4, 1893–
March 3, 1897
Vice Presidents:
Thomas A. Hendricks
(1885–89), Adlai E. Stevenson, Sr. (1893–97)
First Lady:
Frances Folsom
Cleveland, his wife
Nicknames:
Big Steve,
Uncle Jumbo
Died:
June 24, 1908

Benjamin Harrison

Benjamin Harrison, grandson of former President William Henry Harrison, was born into a prominent political family. As president, the younger Harrison created the first Pan-American Conference, which aimed to create good relations between the United States and Latin America. He tried to heal Civil War wounds by giving black Americans the right to vote and appointing Frederick Douglass, a former slave, ambassador to Haiti. He also supported the landmark Sherman Antitrust Act, which prevented giant corporations from achieving unfair business monopolies.

"I believe also in the American opportunity which puts the starry sky above every boy's head, and sets his foot upon a ladder that he may climb until his strength gives out."

23rd

Did You Know?

★ Harrison was the last Civil War general to become president.

★ As president, he spent very little time in the office and usually worked only until noon.

★ He hated to engage in small talk, so people who met him thought he was cold and aloof.

★ Six states—North Dakota, South Dakota, Montana, Washington, Idaho, and Wyoming—were added to the Union during his presidency.

★ His daughter, her husband, and their children lived in the White House.

★ Harrison was only five feet, six inches tall.

★ His wife, Caroline, died just before the end of his presidency. Harrison then remarried and had a daughter who was younger than his grandchildren.

★ The Harrisons had electric lighting installed in the White House but were so afraid to touch the switches that they left the lights on all night.

Born:
August 20, 1833

Birthplace:
North Bend, Ohio

Political Party:
Republican

Term of Office:
March 4, 1889–
March 3, 1893

Vice President:
Levi P. Morton

First Lady:
Caroline Lavinia Scott
Harrison, his wife

Nicknames:
Human Iceberg,
Little Ben

Died:
March 13, 1901

William McKinley

A Life in Brief

William McKinley was a member of the U.S. House of Representatives and governor of Ohio. The United States entered the Spanish-American War during McKinley's term, and upon the U.S. victory, the country received the Philippines, Guam, and Puerto Rico from Spain. McKinley instituted the Open Door policy with China, which encouraged a level playing field among the countries involved in Chinese trade. This move established the foundation for the United States to become a powerful empire.

"That's all a man can hope for during his lifetime— to set an example—and when he is dead, to be an inspiration for history."

25th

Did You Know?

⭐ Both of McKinley's children died as infants.

⭐ His wife, Ida, suffered from epileptic seizures, and McKinley was completely devoted to taking care of her. When a seizure came on, McKinley covered her face to hide her features, protecting her dignity.

⭐ He was the first president to run a "front porch" campaign, staying close to his hometown and traveling very little.

⭐ He was the first president to use the telephone to campaign.

⭐ He wore a pink carnation on his jacket lapel and would give it as a token of his affection to acquaintances.

⭐ McKinley was the first president to ride in an automobile. He was brought to the hospital in an ambulance after Leon F. Czolgosz, an unemployed mill worker, shot him. The president later died of his injuries.

⭐ As he lay dying, McKinley told his attendants to be careful of the way they informed his wife.

Born:
January 29, 1843
Birthplace:
Niles, Ohio
Political Party:
Republican
Term of Office:
March 4, 1897–
September 14, 1901
Vice Presidents:
Garrett Hobard
(1897–99), Theodore
Roosevelt (March
4–September 14, 1901)
First Lady:
Ida Saxton McKinley,
his wife
Nickname:
Wobbly Willie
Died:
September 14, 1901

Theodore Roosevelt

26th

Theodore Roosevelt (signature)

"Speak softly and carry a big stick."

A Life in Brief

Theodore Roosevelt was a popular president who loved controversy and publicity. Prior to serving as president, he was civil service commissioner of New York, president of the New York City Board of Commissioners, and assistant secretary of the Navy. At the start of the Spanish-American War, Roosevelt commanded the First U.S. Volunteer Cavalry, known as the Rough Riders, who led a daring charge on San Juan Hill in Cuba. Roosevelt's role as the leader of the Rough Riders earned him war hero status, and upon returning to New York at the end of the war, he was elected governor. As president, Roosevelt ordered the building of the Panama Canal, which was a tremendous boost to U.S. commerce. He has been ranked by historians as one of the top five presidents of the United States because of his handling of both domestic and foreign policy.

⭐ Roosevelt was a sickly child, but as a teenager, he worked out and became an advocate of exercise.

⭐ He graduated from Harvard.

⭐ The Teddy bear is named for him.

⭐ He wrote more than 30 books.

⭐ At 42 years old when he took office, Roosevelt was the youngest president.

⭐ Roosevelt's first wife, Alice, died during childbirth. His mother died on the same day. Distraught, Roosevelt headed out West, where he spent two years as a cattle rancher and a sheriff in an attempt to recover from the double tragedy.

⭐ He was shot while on the campaign trail but refused medical treatment until after he had given his speech. He spoke for more than an hour, then went to the hospital.

⭐ He was the first president to receive the Nobel Peace Prize.

⭐ Roosevelt was the first leader to take action to preserve wetlands, wildlife refuges, and national forests.

⭐ He was the first president to be photographed in action.

⭐ Roosevelt once participated in a boxing match that left him blind in one eye.

⭐ He considered people of color to be the "white man's burden."

⭐ His six children wreaked havoc in the White House. They brought a pony into the White House elevator, frighted visiting officials with a four-foot-long king snake, and dropped water balloons onto the heads of White House guards.

⭐ In 1909, he went on a safari in Africa, taking home more than 3,000 animal trophies, including elephants, lions, and rhinos.

Born:
October 27, 1858
Birthplace:
New York, New York
Political Party:
Republican
Term of Office:
September 14, 1901–March 3, 1909
Vice President:
Charles W. Fairbanks
First Lady:
Edith Kermit Carow Roosevelt, his second wife
Nickname:
Teddy
Died:
January 6, 1919

Roosevelt and his wife Edith in Africa, 1910

"The only man who makes no mistake is the man who does nothing."

William Howard Taft

27th

W H Taft

"We live in a stage of politics, where legislators seem to regard the passage of laws as much more important than the results of their enforcement."

A Life in Brief

William Howard Taft once said that he felt more at home in the courtroom than the White House. Prior to the presidency, he served as chief civil administrator of the Philippines under President McKinley, and secretary of war under Theodore Roosevelt.

He oversaw the continued building of the Panama Canal and extended statehood to Arizona and New Mexico. In 1921, he became Chief Justice of the Supreme Court.

⭐ Taft graduated from Yale University and practiced law.

⭐ He weighed more than 300 pounds, making him the heaviest president.

⭐ He began the tradition of the president throwing out the first pitch at the start of the baseball season.

⭐ Taft was the first president to take up golf, which caused a surge of interest in the sport across the nation.

⭐ He was the only man to hold the highest executive office (president) and the highest judicial office (Chief Justice of the Supreme Court).

⭐ Taft's wife, Helen, visited Japan and fell in love with the cherry trees there. When she returned to the United States, she had 3,000 cherry trees planted on and around the White House grounds.

⭐ He once got stuck in the White House bathtub and needed six men to help him out.

⭐ He kept a cow, which lived in the garage.

⭐ Taft was president when the *Titanic* sank.

⭐ He was the first president to be buried at Arlington National Cemetery.

⭐ Taft's different approach to the presidency disappointed his predecessor and mentor, Theodore Roosevelt. When Taft was nominated for reelection in 1912, Roosevelt broke with the Republican Party and formed his own, the Bull Moose party.

⭐ Taft often embarrassed his family and colleagues by falling asleep during briefing sessions, cabinet meetings, and concerts.

Born:
September 15, 1857
Birthplace:
Cincinnati, Ohio
Political Party:
Republican
Term of Office:
March 4, 1909–
March 3, 1913
Vice President:
James S. Sherman
First Lady:
Helen "Nellie" Herron Taft, his wife
Nickname:
Big Bill
Died:
March 8, 1930

President Taft, circa 1909–13

Taft speaking from a train near Hutchinson, Kansas

Woodrow Wilson

28th

"We grow great by dreams. All big men are dreamers."

A Life in Brief

Thomas Woodrow Wilson has been named by historians as one of the five most important American presidents, alongside Washington, Lincoln, Theodore Roosevelt, and Franklin D. Roosevelt. Wilson's domestic policies gave the federal government more control over the economy and protected the interests of the country's citizens.

His foreign policy helped to establish a new role for America in the world, and as a result of his efforts as president, the White House became the center of power in Washington.

⭐ Wilson attended Princeton University and received a Ph.D. from Johns Hopkins University.

⭐ He was president of Princeton University in 1902.

⭐ Wilson's second wife, Edith, was a descendant of Pocahontas.

⭐ He was the first sitting president to take a trip to Europe.

⭐ Wilson appointed the first Jewish justice to the Supreme Court.

⭐ He acquired the Virgin Islands for the United States from Denmark.

⭐ Wilson won the Nobel Peace Prize for his commitment to world peace, the second president to receive that honor.

⭐ He proposed many laws designed to improve the quality of life in the country, one of which ended child labor.

⭐ The 17th, 18th, and 19th Amendments to the Constitution were added during Wilson's presidency. Respectively, these amendments allowed for United States citizens to vote for their state senators instead of the senators being appointed; banned all alcoholic beverages (Prohibition); and gave women the right to vote.

⭐ Wilson campaigned against the United States entering the world war that had begun in 1914 but eventually concluded that the country could not remain neutral. On April 2, 1917, the United States entered World War I with a declaration of war on Germany. Wilson defended the United States' entrance into the war as necessary to make the world "safe for democracy."

⭐ He signed bills that included the creation of the Department of Labor, the Federal Reserve, and the Federal Trade Commission.

⭐ During World War I, there was a shortage of workers available to care for the White House lawn. Wilson arranged to have sheep graze on the front lawn in order to keep the grass low. He donated their wool to the Red Cross to help in making the soldiers' uniforms.

⭐ At the end of World War I, he proposed a peace plan that included creating the League of Nations.

Born:
December 28, 1856
Birthplace:
Staunton, Virginia
Political Party:
Democratic
Term of Office:
March 4, 1913–
March 3, 1921
Vice President:
Thomas R. Marshall
First Ladies:
Ellen Louise Axson (1913–14); Edith Bolling Galt (1916–21), his wives
Nickname:
None
Died:
February 3, 1924

President Wilson, circa 1913–1921

Warren G. Harding

A Life in Brief

Warren Gamaliel Harding had a down-home appeal that stemmed from his childhood on the farm. His popularity and honesty earned him political respect. However, as president, Harding preferred to be popular rather than a good leader. He appointed many corrupt cabinet members and prevented America from joining the League of Nations. When he died of a heart attack in his sleep after falling ill from suspected food poisoning, rumors began that his wife had poisoned him to save him from the corruption charges that were overtaking his administration.

Warren G Harding

"Our most dangerous tendency is to expect too much of government, and at the same time do for it too little."

29th

Born:
November 2, 1865
Birthplace:
Corsica (now Blooming Grove), Ohio
Political Party:
Republican
Term of Office:
March 4, 1921–
August 2, 1923
Vice President:
Calvin Coolidge
First Lady:
Florence Kling DeWolfe, his wife
Nickname:
None
Died:
August 2, 1923

Did You Know?

⭐ Harding's campaign slogan was "A Return to Normalcy."

⭐ He was the first president to ride in an automobile to his inauguration.

⭐ Harding was the first president to have a radio in the White House.

⭐ He was the first to have one of his presidential addresses broadcast by radio.

⭐ Harding was the first president for whom women could vote.

⭐ He was the first president to visit Alaska and Canada.

⭐ His wife, Flossie, and several other previous First Ladies campaigned for assistance for war veterans. The women became known as "Flossie's Gang."

⭐ Harding was a musician and once said that he "played every instrument but the slide trombone and the E-flat cornet."

⭐ He once threw a birthday party for his dog, Laddie Boy, who was more popular with the press than he was.

Calvin Coolidge

John Calvin Coolidge became lieutenant governor of Massachusetts and served as Harding's vice president. When he took over the presidency after Harding's death, he kept most of Harding's corrupt cabinet and made a number of poor decisions on domestic issues, which probably contributed to the onset of the Great Depression. Despite the fact that Coolidge himself was a man of integrity, historians consider him one of the country's worst presidents because of his failure to make a strong, positive impact or leave a lasting legacy.

30th

"Character is the only secure foundation of the state."

Did You Know?

⭐ Coolidge's mother and sister died when Coolidge was a teenager.

⭐ His campaign slogan was "Keep Cool with Coolidge."

⭐ As Harding's vice president, Coolidge usually sat silent during cabinet and Senate meetings, which earned him the nickname "Silent Cal."

⭐ Upon the death of President Harding, Coolidge's father, a justice of the peace, administered the oath of office in the middle of the night. After the swearing-in, Coolidge went back to bed.

⭐ He installed a mechanical horse in the White House.

⭐ He had a pet raccoon named Rebecca. He built her a special house and walked her around the White House on a leash.

⭐ A woman once made a bet with Coolidge that she could get him to say more than two words. He replied, "You lose."

Born:
July 4, 1872
Birthplace:
Plymouth Notch, Vermont
Political Party:
Republican
Term of Office:
August 3, 1923–March 3, 1929
Vice President:
Charles G. Dawes
First Lady:
Grace Anna Goodhue Coolidge, his wife
Nickname:
Silent Cal
Died:
January 5, 1933

Herbert Hoover

31st

Herbert Hoover

"A splendid storehouse of integrity and freedom has been bequeathed to us by our forefathers. In this day of confusion, of peril to liberty, our high duty is to see that this storehouse is not robbed of its contents."

A Life in Brief

Herbert Clark Hoover saw financial success early in life. He worked as a mining engineer, and at age 34, he opened his own mining consulting business. During World War I, Hoover was asked by President Wilson to head the U.S. Food Administration. Hoover performed brilliantly, organizing the conservation of resources and supplying American troops and their allies with food. After the war, Hoover continued his efforts to help others as head of the European Relief and Rehabilitation Administration, sending 34 million tons of food, clothing, and medicine to various war-ravaged areas of Europe. Hoover also served as secretary of commerce under Presidents Harding and Coolidge, positions that prepared him to be the Republican nominee for president.

★ Hoover was the first president born west of the Mississippi River.

★ He received more than 50 honorary degrees from American universities.

★ He loved to go fly-fishing.

★ Hoover traveled the world with his wife, Lou.

★ He wrote the leading textbook on mining at the time.

★ Hoover became a millionaire by age 40 and refused to be paid as president. He even gave the presidential yacht to the Navy to use.

★ He became the scapegoat for the Great Depression.

★ Hoover did not believe that it was the government's responsibility to care for the people who were suffering as a result of the stock market crash. Nearly two million men, women, and children roamed the streets of the nation, living in slums called "Hoovervilles" and wrapping themselves in newspapers, or "Hoover blankets."

★ He and his wife often spoke Mandarin Chinese when they didn't want their conversation to be overheard.

★ "The Star-Spangled Banner" was adopted as the country's national anthem during Hoover's administration.

Born:
August 10, 1874
Birthplace:
West Branch, Iowa
Political Party:
Republican
Term of Office:
March 4, 1929–
March 3, 1933
Vice President:
Charles Curtis
First Lady:
Lou Henry Hoover, his wife
Nickname:
The Great Engineer
Died:
October 20, 1964

President Hoover signing the Farm Relief Bill, 1929

Dark Days Ahead

In the 1920s, more than two million Americans invested their life savings in the stock market in the hopes of a large return. Many more threw their money into "get rich quick" schemes, unknowingly getting involved with companies that were not reputable. Stocks lost more than 80 percent of their value, and unemployment soared. Wealthy Americans chose to invest their money instead of spending it, which resulted in a stockpile of goods with no one to buy them. Investors became nervous and tried to sell their stock, but with so many people without money, there were no buyers. Investors simply dumped millions of shares of stock, which caused New York Stock Market to crash in October of 1929. The economy continued to decline during the next couple of years, with millions of people out of money and unable to pay their bills or buy food and other essentials. All of these events led to the Great Depression, which was the worst economic crisis in the nation's history and lasted from 1929 through most of the 1930s. During this time, one in four farms went out of business, 5,000 banks closed, and an average of 100,000 jobs disappeared every week. By 1932, 12 million people—one-quarter of the American workforce—were without jobs.

Franklin D. Roosevelt

32nd

Franklin D. Roosevelt

"The only thing we have to fear is fear itself."

A Life in Brief

Franklin Delano Roosevelt began his political career when he won a seat in the New York State Senate in 1910. Under President Wilson, Roosevelt was assistant secretary of the Navy and helped to ready the country for its entry into World War I. He was elected governor of New York and served two terms, during which time he signed a number of laws designed to help the country recover from the Great Depression. Among his key pieces of legislation were insurance for people who were unemployed and limits on work hours. As part of his campaign for president during the Great Depression, he promised a "New Deal," a series of programs designed to help citizens get back on their feet. The New Deal programs brought about recovery for a weak nation and made Roosevelt extremely popular with the American people. He was so popular that he was elected to an unprecedented four terms in office! His leadership during the worst domestic crisis since the Civil War strengthened the power of the nation and restored honor to the office of the president.

Did You Know?

★ At age five, Roosevelt met then-President Grover Cleveland, who said, "My little man, I am making a strange wish for you. It is that you will never be president of the United States."

★ He attended Harvard University and Columbia Law School.

★ At age 39, Roosevelt contracted polio and lost the use of his legs. He hid his disability so well that many people didn't realize that he was confined to a wheelchair.

★ He had a black Scottish terrier named Fala who went everywhere with him.

★ His German shepherd, Major, bit guests and ripped the pants off the British prime minister.

★ He was a stamp collector and acquired more than 25,000 stamps.

★ Roosevelt was the first president to appoint a woman to a cabinet position: Frances Perkins served as secretary of labor.

★ Prohibition was repealed during his administration.

★ Roosevelt was the first president to appear on television.

★ He used the new medium of radio and held "fireside chats," during which he reassured a nervous nation that the economic crisis would pass.

★ He was the first president whose speech was broadcast in a foreign language (French).

★ After the Japanese bombed Pearl Harbor, Hawaii, on December 7, 1941, Roosevelt declared war on Japan, signaling the entry of the United States in World War II, which lasted until 1945.

Born:
January 30, 1882
Birthplace:
Hyde Park, New York
Political Party:
Democratic
Term of Office:
March 4, 1933–
April 12, 1945
Vice Presidents:
John Garner (1933–37), Henry Wallace (1937–41), Harry S. Truman (1941–45)
First Lady:
Anna Eleanor Roosevelt, his wife
Nickname:
FDR
Died:
April 12, 1945

Part of an impoverished family of nine Depression refugees from Iowa, August 1936

President Roosevelt's funeral procession, April 15, 1945

Harry S. Truman

A Life in Brief

Harry S. Truman began his political career as a judge in Missouri. As vice president, he gained the presidency after Roosevelt died. A man of integrity and honesty, he is considered one of the nation's best presidents. He faced enormous domestic economic challenges and World War II, but he emerged with plans that helped the country to get back on its feet. His Fair Deal helped Americans, the atomic bombs he ordered dropped over Japan ended World War II, and his treaty organizations guarded world peace.

33rd

"America was not built on fear. America was built on courage, on imagination, and an unbeatable determination to do the job at hand."

Born:
May 8, 1884
Birthplace:
Lamar, Missouri
Political Party:
Democratic
Term of Office:
April 12, 1945–
January 20, 1953
Vice Presidents:
John Garner
(1945–49), Alben
Barkley (1949–53)
First Lady:
Elizabeth "Bess"
Virginia Wallace
Truman, his wife
Nickname:
Give 'em Hell Harry
Died:
December 26, 1972

Did You Know?

⭐ Truman's middle initial, S, doesn't stand for anything.

⭐ By the time he was 14 years old, he had read all of the books in his local library.

⭐ He married his childhood sweetheart, Elizabeth Virginia Wallace.

⭐ Truman was a skilled pianist and brought three pianos to the White House.

⭐ His favorite saying was, "If you can't stand the heat, get out of the kitchen."

⭐ Truman was the only president in the 20th century without a college education.

⭐ He was the first president to travel underwater in a submarine.

⭐ He ended segregation in the armed forces.

⭐ In the election of 1948, Truman pulled out a narrow victory in one of the most stunning political comebacks in history.

Dwight D. Eisenhower

Dwight David Eisenhower was one of the nation's greatest military commanders. When the United States entered World War II, Eisenhower received several important command assignments, including Operation Overlord, which was the Allied invasion of Nazi-occupied Europe. He returned home from the war a hero, admired, respected, and immensely popular. These attributes won him the Republican nomination and the presidency twice.

"America is best described by one word, freedom."

34th

Did You Know?

★ The slogan for Eisenhower's 1952 presidential campaign was "I like Ike."

★ He was the only president to serve in both World War I and World War II.

★ He was the first president to obtain a pilot's license.

★ He was the first president to fly in the presidential jet.

★ Eisenhower renamed the presidential retreat Camp David after his grandson.

★ He created the National Aeronautics Space Administration (NASA).

★ He ended the Korean War by negotiating a cease-fire.

★ He did not support the Supreme Court's ruling that segregation in schools was illegal.

★ He got rid of all of the squirrels on the White House lawn because they were destroying his golf green.

★ After he retired, Eisenhower enjoyed painting by numbers.

Born:
October 14, 1890
Birthplace:
Denison, Texas
Political Party:
Republican
Term of Office:
January 20, 1953–
January 20, 1961
Vice President:
Richard M. Nixon
First Lady:
Mary "Mamie" Geneva Doud Eisenhower, his wife
Nickname:
Ike
Died:
March 28, 1969

John F. Kennedy

35th

"And so my fellow Americans, ask not what your country can do for you; ask what you can do for your country."

A Life in Brief

John Fitzgerald Kennedy was born into a family of wealth, prestige, and politics. He served in the U.S. House of Representatives and the U.S. Senate, and during World War II, he was a Naval commander in the South Pacific. When his boat was rammed by a Japanese vessel, Kennedy guided his crew on a three-mile swim to an island for safety. He received the U.S. Navy and Marine Corps Medal for Valor, and a Purple Heart for the injuries that he sustained. The total impact of Kennedy's administration would never be known, however, as he was shot and killed by Lee Harvey Oswald on November 22, 1963, while his motorcade traveled through Dallas, Texas. Kennedy's death was so shocking that many people can recall exactly where they were when they heard the news that he had been shot.

⭐ Kennedy was the first president born in the 20th century and the youngest president to die in office (age 46).

⭐ During his campaign for president in 1960, Kennedy and Republican opponent, Richard Nixon, participated in the first televised debates.

⭐ On April 17, 1961, Kennedy ordered an invasion of Cuba to remove Fidel Castro from power. The invasion team landed at the Bay of Pigs and was defeated by Castro's forces. The White House denied involvement in the failure.

⭐ He received the Pulitzer Prize in history for his book *Profiles in Courage*.

⭐ In October of 1962, the U.S. came frighteningly close to nuclear war with the Soviet Union and Cuba. After 14 tense days, the Soviet Union agreed to dismantle its nuclear weapons if the United States did not invade Cuba, where the Soviet Union's weapons were being built.

⭐ He supported the space program and challenged Americans to put a man on the moon by the end of the decade. The first manned lunar landing occurred on July 20, 1969, but Kennedy wasn't alive to see it.

⭐ He founded the Peace Corps.

⭐ He suffered from back trouble, malaria, and Addison's disease.

⭐ In response to a growing conflict in Vietnam, Kennedy sent 16,000 American Special Forces military advisers to that country to give the South Vietnamese fighters warfare training.

Born:
May 29, 1917
Birthplace:
Brookline, Massachusetts
Political Party:
Democratic
Term of Office:
January 20, 1961–
November 22, 1963
Vice President:
Lyndon B. Johnson
First Lady:
Jacqueline Lee Bouvier Kennedy, his wife
Nicknames:
JFK, Jack
Died:
November 22, 1963

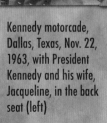

President Kennedy and Mayor Willy Brandt of Berlin at the White House (below)

Kennedy motorcade, Dallas, Texas, Nov. 22, 1963, with President Kennedy and his wife, Jacqueline, in the back seat (left)

Lyndon B. Johnson

36th

"If government is to serve any purpose it is to do for others what they are unable to do for themselves."

A Life in Brief

Lyndon Baines Johnson served in the U.S. House of Representatives and the U.S. Senate. After only five years in the Senate, in 1953, he was named Senate Minority Leader, the youngest senator to hold that honor. A year later, when the Democrats gained control of the Senate, Johnson became Majority Leader. He also served in World War II in the Naval Reserve. Then-President Franklin Roosevelt insisted that all congressmen on active duty in the war be allowed to leave their posts and return to their duties in Washington, and Johnson returned home a hero.

⭐ Everyone in Johnson's immediate family had the initials LBJ.

⭐ Johnson was a poor student in school and did not get into college on his first try.

⭐ Before going off to college, he was arrested for fighting.

⭐ Johnson proposed to his wife, Lady Bird, the day after they met. The two were married three months later.

⭐ His social and economic programs included laws to aid in education finance, fight poverty, and allow everyone the right to vote.

⭐ Johnson was the only president sworn into office on an airplane. He was given the oath of office aboard Air Force One on the afternoon of President Kennedy's assassination.

⭐ He was the first president to appoint an African American to his cabinet and to the Supreme Court.

⭐ During his administration, the Civil Rights Act, the Voting Rights Act, and Medicare all were signed into law.

⭐ President Johnson continued fighting the Vietnam War, but he couldn't win it. In fact, Johnson's popularity sank as numerous antiwar protests broke out around the country and he was unable to devise any sort of plan outlining victory or honorable, timely withdrawal of the troops from Vietnam.

Born:
August 27, 1908
Birthplace:
near Johnson City, Texas
Political Party:
Democratic
Term of Office:
November 22, 1963–
January 20, 1969
Vice President:
Hubert H. Humphrey
First Lady:
Claudia "Lady Bird" Alta Taylor Johnson, his wife
Nickname:
LBJ
Died:
January 22, 1973

President Johnson signing Civil Rights Bill, April 11, 1968

Sen. Lyndon B. Johnson, Senate Majority Leader, 1955

Richard Nixon

37th

"This office is a sacred trust and I am determined to be worthy of that trust."

A Life in Brief

Richard Milhous Nixon is probably best known for his involvement in the Watergate scandal and his resignation from the presidency that followed. But prior to the scandal that ruined his political career, Nixon had great successes in politics. He was elected to both the U.S. House of Representatives and the U.S. Senate, and he served as vice president when Eisenhower was in office. After an unsuccessful bid for the presidency in 1960, he was elected president in 1968 and reelected in 1972.

Did You Know?

- Nixon was a Naval officer in the Pacific in World War II.

- After college, he applied to become an agent in the Federal Bureau of Investigation (FBI) but wasn't accepted.

- He created the Environmental Protection Agency (EPA).

- Nixon was an excellent poker player.

- He liked to play the piano and often invited guests to sing along.

- He met his future wife, Patricia, at a community theater group.

- Nixon lost his bid to become governor of California in 1962.

- He was the first president to visit all 50 states.

- Nixon was the first president to travel to China. His visit opened up communication with that country and helped to promote goodwill between the U.S. and China.

- He ended the military draft.

- In the election of 1972, Nixon won 49 of 50 states, losing only in Massachusetts.

- He had a reputation of running attack ads against his political competitors. One opponent called him "Tricky Dick," and the nickname stuck.

- Nixon was granted a full pardon for his involvement in the Watergate scandal by his successor, Gerald R. Ford.

Born:
January 9, 1913
Birthplace:
Yorba Linda, California
Political Party:
Republican
Term of Office:
January 20, 1969–
August 9, 1974
Vice Presidents:
Spiro T. Agnew
(1969–73); Gerald R.
Ford (1973–74)
First Lady:
Thelma "Patricia"
Catherine Ryan Nixon,
his wife
Nickname:
Tricky Dick
Died:
April 22, 1994

President Nixon, circa 1969–74

The Watergate Scandal

When Nixon ran for reelection in 1972, he authorized his advisers to do many illegal things in order to stay a step ahead of the Democrats. His officials were caught breaking into the Watergate Hotel, where the Democratic National Committee had its election headquarters. Many of Nixon's officers resigned, and some were convicted of trying to cover up the incident. Nixon denied involvement at first, but he was forced to turn over several tape recordings that proved he knew what was going on. Before he could be impeached, or brought up on charges, Nixon resigned from office, becoming the first president to do so.

Gerald Ford

38th

Gerald R. Ford

"A government big enough to give you everything you want is a government big enough to take from you everything you have."

A Life in Brief

Gerald Rudolph Ford seemed to be the perfect choice to fill the role of president after Richard Nixon resigned. The country was shaken by the Watergate accusations, and Ford was an honest, decent man who was respected by the American people. He served in World War II as a Navy combat officer, and upon returning home from the war, Ford decided to get involved in politics.

He served as a member of the House of Representatives for 25 years, and for a time, he was House Minority Leader. Ford turned 92 years old in 2005 and continued to participate in the activities of the Gerald R. Ford Foundation and his Presidential Library and Museum until his death in 2006.

Did You Know?

- Ford was born Leslie Lynch King, Jr.

- He learned at age 15 that he was adopted.

- Ford was a star football player at the University of Michigan. He received offers from the Detroit Lions and the Green Bay Packers to play professional football.

- In 1963, then-President Lyndon Johnson appointed Ford to the Warren Commission to investigate the death of President Kennedy.

- He was the first president to visit Japan.

- In 1975, he survived two assassination attempts, both by women.

- If meetings in the Oval Office lasted too long, Ford used his golden retriever, Liberty, to break things up.

- He published a book about the Kennedy assassination called *Portrait of an Assassin* and his memoirs titled *A Time to Heal*.

- Ford was president during the country's bicentennial (200-year) celebration on July 4, 1976.

- He was the first president to hire a professional joke writer.

- Ford received the Presidential Medal of Freedom for his efforts to bring the country back together after the Watergate affair.

- Ford lost popular support when he pardoned Nixon for his involvement in the Watergate scandal. Americans mistakenly saw it as a sign Ford had been involved, too.

- He lost more support when he wasn't able to bring the country out of economic recession.

- Ford became known as a klutz after he was caught on camera falling down.

Born:
July 14, 1913
Birthplace:
Omaha, Nebraska
Political Party:
Republican
Term of Office:
August 9, 1974–
January 20, 1977
Vice President:
Nelson A. Rockefeller
First Lady:
Elizabeth "Betty" Boomer Ford, his wife
Nickname:
Jerry
Died:
December 26, 2006

President Ford (left) aboard Air Force One during a campaign trip in the South

President Ford appearing at the House Judiciary Subcommittee hearing on pardoning former President Richard Nixon, Washington, D.C.

Jimmy Carter

39th

"We must adjust to changing times and still hold to unchanging principles."

A Life in Brief

James Earl Carter, Jr. enrolled in the United States Naval Academy, and upon graduation, signed on to be an officer in the Navy's first experimental nuclear submarine. He served as governor of Georgia and won a seat on the state senate. As president, Carter negotiated the Camp David Accords, an historic peace agreement between Israel and Egypt. He also established a "superfund" to clean up environmental disasters, and he helped found Habitat for Humanity, which builds houses for people who are less fortunate. He also succeeded in establishing excellent trade relations with China. Today, Carter continues to serve as ambassador for various international missions, as well as advises presidents on Middle East and human rights issues.

Born:
October 1, 1924
Birthplace:
Plains, Georgia
Political Party:
Democrat
Term of Office:
January 20, 1977–
January 20, 1981
Vice President:
Walter F. Mondale
First Lady:
Eleanor Rosalynn Smith
Carter, his wife
Nickname:
Jimmy

- Carter was the first president born in a hospital.

- He grew up in a house that didn't have electricity or indoor plumbing.

- He was a fierce opponent of segregation, and as a representative on the Georgia state senate, he helped to repeal laws that prevented blacks from voting.

- Carter built a tree house for his daughter, Amy, on the White House grounds.

- The Department of Energy was created during his term.

- Carter was the first president sworn in under his nickname (Jimmy).

- The country experienced its largest inflation increase since 1946 during Carter's term.

- He often had trouble getting Congress to pass his legislation.

- He won the Nobel Peace Prize in 2002 for his humanitarian efforts.

- Carter's family was involved in several scandals, including one in which his brother Billy received a mysterious $250,000 payment from the government of Libya.

- Carter's presidency was doomed when 50 Americans were taken hostage at the embassy in Iran. A failed rescue attempt assured him that he would not win reelection. The hostages were freed the day Ronald Reagan (the 40th president) was inaugurated.

- He was the first president since 1932 to lose his bid for reelection.

- Under Carter's direction, the U.S. boycotted the 1980 Summer Olympics to protest the Soviet invasion of Afghanistan. America felt the boycott hurt its athletes more than the Soviet Union.

President Carter departing the White House for Camp David, Maryland, circa 1977–81

Carter (center) on a campaign stop at his brother Billy's gas station in Plains, Georgia, Sept. 10, 1976

Ronald Reagan

40th

Ronald Reagan

"America is too great for small dreams."

A Life in Brief

Ronald Wilson Reagan was a successful Hollywood actor whose acting career fueled his political career. He became one of the most recognizable faces in America. He was elected governor of California in 1966, and after watching American confidence dwindle as the result of a struggling economy and soaring inflation, he set his sights on the presidency. Reagan defeated then-President Jimmy Carter in a landslide and began what he called the "Reagan revolution of 1980." As president, he planned to overhaul the government. His successful legislation included allowing for the largest tax cuts in history and increasing military spending that led to the largest military buildup during peacetime in the nation's history.

Did You Know?

- Reagan acted in more than 50 movies.

- He once worked as a sports announcer.

- He served as governor of California for two terms.

- He was the only actor to serve as president.

- At 69, he was the oldest man elected president.

- Less than three months into his first term, Reagan was shot by John Hinckley, a mentally disturbed man, but survived.

- Reagan loved jelly beans. The Jelly Belly® brand created the blueberry flavor just for him so that he could have red, white, and blue jelly beans at his inaugural party.

- His ranch was named Rancho del Cielo, which means "farm of the sky."

- He and his wife, Nancy, jointly won the Congressional Medal of Honor.

- Reagan was the first president to appoint a woman, Sandra Day O'Connor, to the Supreme Court.

- One of his foreign policy slogans was "Peace Through Strength."

- Reagan and then-Soviet leader Mikhail Gorbachev together took the first steps toward ending the Cold War.

- During his presidency, the country accumulated more debt than during all the previous presidents' terms put together.

Born:
February 6, 1911
Birthplace:
Tampico, Illinois
Political Party:
Republican
Term of Office:
January 20, 1981–
January 20, 1989
Vice President:
George H. W. Bush
First Lady:
Nancy Davis Reagan, his wife
Nickname:
The Great Communicator
Died:
June 5, 2004

The Iran-Contra Affair

In 1985, President Reagan approved a secret deal to sell U.S. missiles to Iran in exchange for seven American hostages who had been captured during President Carter's term and were being held in Lebanon. This contradicted Reagan's publicly stated policy that the United States did not bargain with terrorists. Reagan initially denied that the deal ever occurred, but he took back his statement a week later. However, he insisted that the exchange had not been an "arms-for-hostages" deal, but rather an attempt to improve relations with Iran and Lebanon.

President Reagan (right) with Republican Senator Dan Quayle at the White House, 1987

George Bush

41ST

George Bush

"If anyone tells you that America's best days are behind her, they're looking the wrong way."

A Life in Brief

George Herbert Walker Bush was born into a privileged family in suburban Massachusetts. He received the Distinguished Flying Cross and three Air Medals for his bravery in service as a Naval pilot during World War II. After returning home from the war, he worked as an oil field supply salesman, and by the age of 30, he was co-founder of three oil companies. After an unsuccessful run at the U.S. Senate, he was elected to the U.S. House of Representatives. International affairs became the focus of his political life: He served as ambassador to the United Nations and U.S. envoy to China. During his presidency, several important pieces of legislation were passed. Among those are the Americans with Disabilities Act, which prevented companies from discriminating against people with disabilities, and the Clean Air Act, which was an effort to control the amount of pollution released into the air.

Did You Know?

Born:
June 12, 1924
Birthplace:
Milton, Massachusetts
Political Party:
Republican
Term of Office:
January 20, 1989–
January 20, 1993
Vice President:
J. Danforth Quayle
First Lady:
Barbara Pierce Bush,
his wife
Nickname:
Poppy

⭐ Just a few days before turning 19, Bush became the youngest Naval aviator up to that time.

⭐ Bush was the first president who had been the head of the Central Intelligence Agency (CIA).

⭐ He is related to presidents Pierce, Lincoln, Theodore Roosevelt, and Ford.

⭐ He played baseball at Yale University and kept his glove in his desk in the Oval Office.

⭐ Bush challenged then-Soviet leader Mikhail Gorbachev to a game of horseshoes, which Gorbachev had never played before. Gorbachev threw a "ringer" (when the horseshoe encircles the post) on his first toss.

⭐ He hated broccoli so much that he did not allow it in the White House.

⭐ After announcing, "Read my lips, no new taxes" at the 1988 Republican Convention, Bush raised taxes.

⭐ He sent American troops into Panama to topple General Manuel Noriega's corrupt regime.

⭐ In 1991, Bush entered the Persian Gulf War in an effort to defend Kuwait.

At Islamorada in the Florida Keys, Bush still hosts his own fishing tournament.

⭐ He went skydiving for his 80th birthday.

⭐ At a state dinner in 1992, Bush had the flu. In full view of cameras, he vomited on the Prime Minister of Japan, then fainted. At a later state dinner for Japan, Bush joked, "This time, dinner is on me."

President Bush, 1989

Bill Clinton

42nd

"We need a spirit of community, a sense that we are all in this together. If we have no sense of community, the American dream will wither."

A Life in Brief

William Jefferson Clinton knew at a young age that he wanted to be involved in politics. He even began collecting books about the presidents as a child. In 1974, he became state attorney general of Arkansas after an unsuccessful run at a seat in the U.S. House of Representatives. He became governor of Arkansas in 1978 and served for several terms, after which time he set his sights on the White House. After he won the 1992 presidential election, one of his main goals was to improve the sluggish economy, which he did with incredible success. The country enjoyed the lowest unemployment rates in modern times, the lowest inflation rates in 30 years, and low crime rates. He also signed legislation designed to provide economic relief to the middle class and ensure equal employment and educational rights for every citizen. In 2001, after having served two terms as president, Clinton left the White House with a historically high job approval rating.

Did You Know?

★ As a young man, Clinton met and had a picture taken with then-President Kennedy.

★ He protested the Vietnam War while he was a student at Oxford University in London, England.

★ Clinton is an excellent saxophone player and once even considered becoming a professional musician.

★ The family pets included a Labrador named Buddy and a cat named Socks.

★ He is a Rhodes Scholar and a graduate of Yale University Law School.

★ At age 32, he was the youngest governor in Arkansas history.

★ He negotiated successful peace talks between Protestants and Catholics in Northern Ireland.

★ Clinton directed peace talks between Israel and the Palestinian Liberation Organization (PLO).

★ He organized the North American Free Trade Agreement (NAFTA) with Canada and Mexico.

★ He successfully worked with NATO to stop Serbia from killing Muslims in Bosnia.

★ Clinton earned the nickname "Slick Willy" because he often changed his mind on issues.

★ He and his wife, Hillary, created a universal health care plan, but the bill was not approved by Congress.

★ He was the second president to face impeachment by the House of Representatives. He was charged with lying under oath and obstructing justice, but the Senate did not convict him.

Born:
August 19, 1946
Birthplace:
Hope, Arkansas
Political Party:
Democrat
Term of Office:
January 20, 1993–January 20, 2001
Vice President:
Al Gore, Jr.
First Lady:
Hillary Rodham Clinton, his wife
Nicknames:
Slick Willy, Bill

President Clinton, 1992

George W. Bush

43rd

"I was not elected to serve one party, but one nation."

A Life in Brief

George Walker Bush was born into a family where his father was and brother would also become involved in politics. Bush worked on his father's successful 1988 presidential campaign, and shortly after, he and several other partners purchased the Texas Rangers professional baseball team, of which he was part owner until 1998. He was elected governor of Texas in 1994 and served in that role for six years. In 2000, he set his sights on the White House. He won the longest and closest presidential election in history, beating out Al Gore, Jr., in a decision that was eventually made by a 5-4 Supreme Court vote. He was president when the United States was attacked by terrorists on September 11, 2001, and after that attack, Bush created the office of Homeland Security in an effort to improve protection of Americans and restore the public's shaken confidence. He also declared an international "War on Terror" in the hopes of rounding up Osama bin Laden, who is believed to have been behind the September 11 attacks. Convinced that Iraqi dictator Saddam Hussein was hiding biological and chemical weapons, Bush authorized the U.S. invasion of Iraq, taking the nation to war in March 2003.

Born:
July 6, 1946
Birthplace:
New Haven, CT
Political Party:
Republican
Term of Office:
January 20, 2001–present
Vice President:
Dick Cheney
First Lady:
Laura Welch Bush, his wife
Nickname:
Dubya ("W")

★ After his sister, Robin, died at age three, Bush took it upon himself to try to cheer up his parents. He became known as something of a performer as he tried out his jokes on his family.

★ He was head football cheerleader in high school.

★ After college, Bush joined the Texas Air National Guard, where he trained on F-102 fighters.

★ He and his wife, Laura, married three months after meeting on a date that friends had arranged.

★ Bush and his wife have two daughters, Barbara and Jenna, who are named after their grandmothers.

★ The family pets include two dogs, Barney and Miss Beazley, a cat, Willie, and a cow named Ophelia.

★ Bush has collected over 250 autographed baseballs.

★ During his term as governor of Texas, air quality in that state became the worst in the nation.

★ His brother, Jeb, was elected governor of Florida in 1999.

★ Bush was the first president to give the role of secretary of state to a black American. Colin Powell served in the first Bush administration from January 2001 until January 2005.

★ He ran for reelection in 2004 against John Kerry and became president for a second term.

★ He once repaired his broken bed with neckties.

★ His Texas ranch is known as the "Texas White House" or the "Western White House."

White House, earliest known view, **circa 1860s**

Present-day White House

Index